STARTING OUT

SNOWMOBILES

LORI DITTMER

CREATIVE EDUCATION • CREATIVE PAPERBACKS

CONT

ENTS

I AM A SNOWMOBILE.

My skis glide across ice and snow.

Look at my handlebars and my track!

A rider sits on the seat. Sometimes, they stand to see farther.

My bumpy track grips the snow. My engine makes me go. Vroom!

I travel on trails. I race up

and down hills.

I can go up to 120 miles (193 km) per hour!

My lights show others I am near.

I slow to a stop with my brake.

I explore remote places.

Let's go sledding again!

MAKE A NOISE

RRAAAP!

Can you make the sounds of a snowmobile? They roar, whir, and rumble.

Listen to these sounds:

Now it is your turn!

SNOWMOBILE WORDS

Glide: To move smoothly

Remote: An area that is hard to get to

Track: The rubber belt that moves a snowmobile forward

READING CORNER

Arnold, Quinn M. *Snowmobiles*. Mankato, Minn.: Creative Education and Creative Paperbacks, 2020.

Stevens, Craig. *Snowmobile Mania*. New York: Crabtree Publishing, 2022.

Walker, Hubert. *Snowmobiling*. Mendota Heights, Minn.: Apex Editions, 2022.

INDEX

PUBLISHED BY CREATIVE EDUCATION AND CREATIVE PAPERBACKS
P.O. Box 227, Mankato, Minnesota 56002
Creative Education and Creative Paperbacks are imprints of The Creative Company
www.thecreativecompany.us

LIBRARY OF CONGRESS CATALOGING-IN-PUBLICATION DATA
Names: Dittmer, Lori author
Title: Snowmobiles / Lori Dittmer.
Description: Mankato, Minnesota : Creative Education and Creative Paperbacks, [2026] | Series: Starting out | Includes bibliographical references and index. | Audience: Ages 4-7 | Audience: Grades K-1 | Summary: "Introduce beginning readers to a day on the slopes with a snowmobile in this STEM starter. Includes photos, a labeled vehicle diagram, "Make a Noise" section, glossary, and further resources"— Provided by publisher.
Identifiers: LCCN 2025013189 (print) | LCCN 2025013190 (ebook) | ISBN 9798895810293 library binding | ISBN 9781682779828 paperback | ISBN 9798895811559 ebook
Subjects: LCSH: Snowmobiles—Juvenile literature | Snowmobiling—Juvenile literature | CYAC: Snowmobiles | Snowmobiling
Classification: LCC TL234.2 .D57 2026 (print) | LCC TL234.2 (ebook) | DDC 629.228/8--dc23/eng/20250424
LC record available at https://lccn.loc.gov/2025013189
LC ebook record available at https://lccn.loc.gov/2025013190

DESIGN AND PRODUCTION
Design by Rhea Magaro
Art direction by Graham Morgan

PHOTOGRAPHS BY
Freepik/Onestock, 11; Getty Images/KKIDD, 2, Per Breiehagen, 10, Richard Hamilton Smith, 9; Pexels/DIANNA CUDWORTH, 8, Jarod Lovekamp, 4, Osman Arabacı, 12, Sebastian Voortman, 6, Shelly Ohlsson, 14; Shutterstock/Cristian_Nastase, cover; Unsplash/Nate Johnston, 7, Troy Spoelma, 5

Printed in the United States